CW01512635

Original title:
Umbral Gnats Beyond the Mermaid Hulk

Copyright © 2025 Swan Charm

Author: Kene Elistrand
ISBN HARDBACK: 978-1-80562-457-8
ISBN PAPERBACK: 978-1-80563-978-7

The Shimmering Abyss of Secrets

In the depths where shadows creep,
Whispers of lost dreams softly seep.
Glimmers dance in the velvet night,
Secrets guard their fleeting light.

Bubbles rise from the ocean floor,
Carrying tales of those before.
Old and wise, the depths do keep,
A shimmering abyss, dark but deep.

Gaze into waters so profound,
Mysteries swirl, lost and found.
Echoes of laughter, tears, and strife,
Secrets woven into each life.

Dare you dive into the unknown?
Where treasures and dangers have grown.
With courage close and fear at bay,
Discover the truths hidden away.

Each ripple tells a story grand,
In the heart of a secret land.
Follow the light, follow the sound,
In the abyss, new worlds abound.

Enchanted Currents of Dusk

As day retreats, the dusk arrives,
Crickets sing while firefly thrives.
Currents whisper through the trees,
With every breath, a gentle tease.

Golden hues begin to fade,
Casting spells in twilight's glade.
Under the stars, the magic swells,
Each moment tells the tale it tells.

Waves of dreams drift on the breeze,
Carried far with such sweet ease.
In this twilight, secrets wane,
Enchanted thoughts like softest rain.

With shadows thick and twilight's sigh,
The world is wrapped in a gentle lie.
Cloaked in mystery, night's parade,
Where hopes are born and fears delayed.

So let the currents guide your way,
Through whispered dreams till break of day.
In the calm embrace of night's soft kiss,
Find your heart in the starlit bliss.

Veils of the Mysterious Deep

Beneath the waves, the veils reside,
Guardians of secrets they abide.
Whispers of ancient tides they weave,
In depths where few would dare to leave.

Fathoms deep where silence reigns,
Dancing shadows, forgotten chains.
The waters cradle thoughts unspoken,
A mysterious bond, forever broken.

In the dark, the sirens sing,
Bringing dreams on gossamer wing.
With every plunge, a story set,
In the tranquil deep, we won't forget.

Veils obscure the treasures near,
Where hope entwines with growing fear.
Journey forth into the night,
Embrace the veils, seek the light.

For within the unknown, magic blooms,
In hidden depths where starlust looms.
Veiled in mystery, secrets keep,
Awakening truths from the ancient deep.

Beneath the Lurking Shadows

In the corner of your mind's eye,
Lurking shadows drift and sigh.
Haunting echoes, a soft call,
Whispers rise, then gently fall.

Beneath the cloak of hidden night,
Darkness dances, a flickered light.
Questions linger, answers hide,
In shadowed corners, dreams abided.

Fears may linger, doubts arise,
But embers spark beneath the skies.
Foes may lurk but friends are near,
In shadows cast, find what is dear.

With each heartbeat, shadows shift,
In the stillness, spirits lift.
Embrace the night, let go the day,
For beneath the lurking, find your way.

Trust the journey, let it unfold,
In whispered tales of brave and bold.
The shadows guard not just despair,
But treasures found when hearts lay bare.

Celestial Mysteries in the Abyss

Beneath the stars of midnight hue,
Whispers echo, secrets few.
In shadows deep where shadows dwell,
The cosmos spins a silent spell.

Waves of light dance, shimmer bright,
In tangled dark, they weave the night.
Forgotten realms of dreams untold,
In celestial hands, the fates unfold.

A tapestry of time and space,
In cosmic depths, a hidden trace.
Where stardust trails meet ocean's tide,
Mysteries of the heart abide.

Galaxies twirl in silent grace,
Every ripple a soft embrace.
With every glance from least to most,
We seek our place, we roam, we coast.

In the abyss, we find our way,
Guided softly by starry play.
The night reveals what day conceals,
In whispered dreams, our truth reveals.

Harmony in the Veil of Water

In liquid realms where silence sings,
Ripples weave through time like strings.
A lullaby of softest waves,
In watery depths, the wonder braves.

The dance of light on surface bright,
Crystals shimmer, a joyful sight.
Within the depths, a world unseen,
Where secrets swim in shades of green.

Gentle sighs of ocean's breath,
In harmony there is no death.
The songs of tides, a soft refrain,
In rhythmic beats, we drown our pain.

Beneath the azure, dreams take flight,
A ballet spun in liquid light.
Where every bubble tells a tale,
In water's arms, we shall not fail.

The veil of water, calm and deep,
In its embrace, our hearts shall leap.
For in the flow, we find our muse,
In harmony, we softly choose.

Ocean's Secret Marionettes

In depths where shadows ebb and flow,
The puppets dance, put on a show.
Silk and seaweed twist and twirl,
As ancient tales begin to whirl.

Impulsive seas, a stage of blue,
Each wave a whisper, each tide a cue.
With strings of coral, they glide with grace,
The ocean's heart, a secret place.

Moonlit beams can pull the strings,
On mossy floors, the shadow flings.
Bemused by waves and tempests' roar,
These marionettes, forevermore.

A curtain drawn of salty mist,
Entwining fate, a lover's tryst.
In every splash,
an echo starts,
The ocean's groove, it knows our hearts.

The secret dance beneath the waves,
In soggy dreams, the spirit braves.
We witness wonder, never fret,
In ocean's grasp, we won't forget.

The Allure of Lurking Legends

In whispered tales of moonlit streams,
Legends linger, clothed in dreams.
The shadows play, a haunting sight,
With sharpened fangs, they blend with night.

They weave a web of cryptic lore,
In echoing woods, forever more.
Ancient spirits arise from dust,
In their embrace, we place our trust.

Haunted paths of silver mist,
Allure of stories too sweet to resist.
Each winding road, a lured embrace,
In legendary hearts, we find our place.

With flickering firelight, shadows dance,
An unbroken code, a fateful chance.
In grails of gold and thorns of night,
We seek the truth, we chase the light.

The allure of legends calls us near,
With every story, a whispered fear.
In depths of night, the secrets flow,
In lurking tales, we bravely go.

Secrets Beneath the Celestial Swell

Beneath the stars where whispers weave,
The tales of dreams begin to breathe.
In twilight's arms, the secrets hide,
The ocean's song, our hearts abide.

With every wave, a story spun,
Of lost explorers, battles won.
The tides they tell, the winds they share,
In hidden depths, enchantments flare.

A shimmer bright, a glistening trace,
Like shadows dancing in the space.
The moonlit guide, so tender, wise,
Reveals the truth before our eyes.

Yet in the depths, where dangers lie,
A tempest roars, the answers cry.
For secrets kept in water's keep,
Will stir the souls from restless sleep.

So sail along the silver seam,
Where hope and mystery convene.
And find within, the light must dwell,
The magic bright beneath the swell.

The Luminous Abyss

In waters deep where shadows sing,
A world awaits, a whispered thing.
The darkness pools, a velvet sea,
Yet light persists, a mystery.

The glowing creatures dance and sway,
Their luminescence leads the way.
A hidden realm, a treasure trove,
In depths where dreams and wonders rove.

Each shimmering spark, a tale untold,
Of bravery fierce and hearts of gold.
The abyss holds secrets in its fold,
Of ancient magic, brave and bold.

With every tide, the stories teem,
In every wave, a fleeting dream.
The ocean breathes, eternally,
A luminous world, wild and free.

So dive beneath the moon's soft gaze,
And find the truth in darkened bays.
For in the depths where wonders kiss,
Lies the beauty of the luminous abyss.

Nocturnal Echoes of the Surf

When night wraps tight the wandering shore,
And waves recall their timeless lore,
The echoes rise, a haunting tune,
Beneath the watchful, silver moon.

Each crash and sigh, a whisper's flight,
Of distant lands, in dreams of night.
The currents speak of ages past,
Of lovers lost and die-hard cast.

And every swell, a story weaves,
In darkened foam the heart believes.
As seas conspire with the breeze,
To share their secrets with such ease.

A nightingale calls from hidden glen,
Where nature blurs the lines of men.
The surf repeats its melodic dance,
A nocturnal echo, a wistful chance.

So linger long where shadows play,
And hear the calls of night and day.
For in the surf, a song set free,
The whispers blend with infinity.

Shadows Beneath the Sail

The ship cuts through the silken sea,
With sails that gleam, a wild decree.
Yet shadows lurk beneath the hull,
Secrets thrive where silence is full.

With gentle winds that twist and soar,
The ocean sings to those who explore.
A symphony of waves bestowed,
As tales of yore begin to flow.

The compass spins, the stars align,
In every heart, a quest divine.
Yet shadows dance with every swell,
Bearing stories only time can tell.

So whisper low, and heed the call,
For shadows move and shadows fall.
In every knot and every thread,
Lie echoes of the brave and dead.

With courage, sail through darkened night,
And seek the truth in flick'ring light.
For under sails, where dreams prevail,
Are shadows woven with a tale.

Secrets Hidden in Ocean's Shade

Beneath the waves, where whispers lie,
Echoes of dreams in shadows sigh,
Secrets woven in currents deep,
Guardians of the silence keep.

Colors dance in the twilight gleam,
Hidden tales that drift and stream,
Stars aligned in the ocean's heart,
A mystical world, a work of art.

Fathoms below, a treasure trove,
Of wonders that the deep behove,
Crimson corals and shimmered shells,
Each one a story, each one tells.

Moonlit beams on the surface play,
Guiding sailors who lose their way,
With ancient stars as their kin,
They dare to seek what lies within.

In the depth where the shadows roam,
The ocean whispers, "Welcome home."
For every secret, a tale is spun,
A dance of magic, forever begun.

The Melodies of Midnight Whirlpools

Under the moon's beguiling light,
Whirlpools sing through the veil of night,
Notes like whispers in currents sway,
A haunting echo that fades away.

Crescent shadows in a grand ballet,
Stars align as they twist and play,
Water's rhythm, a siren's call,
Ensnaring hearts where the waters fall.

In the depths where the dark tides churn,
Chapters of fate, the lost will yearn,
Melodies weave tales of old,
History etched in waves so bold.

With every swell, a story drifts,
Time entwined in nautical gifts,
The ocean hums a lullaby,
To weary souls who sail on high.

Amidst the ebb of the sea's embrace,
The midnight whirlpool hides its grace,
In every swirl, a dream takes flight,
Suspending moments in the night.

Reflections of Gloomy Reflections

In the glassy stillness of a stormy sea,
Gloomy reflections whisper to me,
Faces of ancients in tides that weep,
Echoes of sorrows in waters deep.

Enigmas linger beneath the gray,
Shadows dance as the waters sway,
Carried by winds of forgotten lore,
Each ripple brings tales from the shore.

Mists of twilight cloak the past,
Haunting reminders that hold us fast,
In depths uncharted, secrets dwell,
Gloomy reflections, a silent spell.

For time is but a fleeting strand,
Captured in waves, not in our hand,
In mirrored depths where dreams collide,
Gloomy reflections shall abide.

Yet amidst the shadows, hope may gleam,
A flicker of light in a silent dream,
We navigate through the veils of time,
Finding our way to the sublime.

The Abyssal Waltz of Shades

In the abyss where the shadows play,
Twilight dips in a waltz of gray,
The dance of specters, soft and slow,
With secrets buried where few may go.

Beneath the waves, a rhythm calls,
As darkness weaves through ancient halls,
The echoes of lives long passed away,
Twist and twirl in the ocean's sway.

Veiled in silence, each step a trace,
Of fleeting moments in this dark place,
Through currents deep, the waltz unfurls,
Vital tales of the sea's lost pearls.

Glimmers of light amidst the dark,
Flickering shadows like a hopeful spark,
In the ocean's arms, we shall find,
The mystic dance that ties mankind.

As tides enchant and moonbeams glide,
The abyssal waltz our hearts collide,
In the ocean's embrace, forever free,
We dive into depths of mystery.

Whispers of Shadow Swarm

In the deep of night where secrets dwell,
Shadows whisper tales they never tell.
Lurking in corners, dark and forlorn,
The shadows creep forth, a new world born.

A rustling breeze stirs ancient dread,
Echoes of whispers where angels tread.
Delicate murmurs, a spell is cast,
Binding the future to shadows of past.

With unseen fingers, they cradle the air,
Painting the silence with strokes of despair.
Yet in their embrace, a promise resides,
For in every dark, a light still abides.

Beware of the swarm that tugs at your heart,
They dance in a rhythm, a haunting art.
But listen, dear child, hold firm to your light,
For shadows can flee with the grace of your might.

Flickering Light beneath the Tide

Beneath the waves, where the lost dreams go,
Flickering lights weave a tale of woe.
Glimmers of hope in the ocean's embrace,
Guide weary souls to a faraway place.

The moon whispers secrets to deep waters dark,
Swaying soft seaweed where once lay a spark.
Rippling currents echo a mystical song,
Calling forth creatures in the sea all along.

In depths of despair, a shimmer remains,
Tales of adventures lie deep in the veins.
Rays of the sun pierce through the cold dread,
Each flicker a promise that hope isn't dead.

So dive into waters, embrace the unknown,
For light hides in shadows, in darkness it's sewn.
Swim true to the tune of forgotten delight,
Unlocking the magic of flickering light.

Chimeras of the Gloom

In the realm of twilight, chimeras arise,
With ghostly faces and haunting cries.
They curl 'round the corners of what we hold dear,
Feeding on whispers, igniting our fear.

Gloom shrouds the path where the lost shadows tread,
Each step holds a promise that dances with dread.
Visions of wonder entwined with despair,
Around every crevice, the chimeras stare.

Yet in the gloom, there's a flicker of grace,
A soft, gentle light in this shadowed space.
For every chimera that lurks in the night,
A spark of resilience can summon the light.

Brave hearts should gather, banish the phantoms,
With laughter and courage, fortify realms.
For chimeras may dwell in the depths of our mind,
But truth is our armor, let's leave them behind.

Dancers of the Lost Lagoon

By the edge of waters where twilight glows,
Dancers of magic embrace river flows.
Their laughter like ripples, soft whispers collide,
In the lost lagoon where secrets abide.

Woven in moonlight, they pirouette free,
Carving their stories with grace by the sea.
Each twirl a reflection of dreams long ago,
Unfolding the beauty in the currents that flow.

With petals of silver, they brush through the night,
Calling the stars with their celestial light.
In this enchanted ballet, we're lost in their trance,
Beneath the veil of the lagoon's mystic dance.

So join in their revels, let cares drift away,
For in every dance, there's magic to sway.
With hearts intertwined, we'll flow with the tide,
In the dancers' embrace, let our spirits reside.

Tidal Dreams of Enchanted Beings

Upon the shores where shadows blend,
Whispers of magic in the wind,
Ocean's tide, a gentle embrace,
Dreams of beings we long to trace.

Colors dance in the moonlit spray,
Secrets held where the mermaids play,
Shells of silver, tales untold,
Woven in currents, brave and bold.

Bubbles rise with laughter's sound,
Lost treasures in the depths abound,
Stars above, like fireflies bright,
Guide our hearts through the velvety night.

Waves sing songs of ancient lore,
Echoes linger on the shore,
Enchanted realms just out of sight,
Awaken dreams with morning light.

In tidal pools where wonders gleam,
A fleeting glimpse of a forgotten dream,
Every crest, a new start,
Living secrets in each heart.

Chants from the Aquatic Beyond

From deep abyss, the voices soar,
In rhythmic waves, they call for more.
A symphony of silvered tones,
Resounds among the ocean's groans.

With every crest, a tale retold,
Of brave adventurers, wise and bold.
Through tides that twist and twirl in dance,
The waters weave a timeless romance.

Enchanting echoes fill the night,
As phantoms of the sea take flight.
They summon tales of love and dread,
In currents strong where dreams are fed.

Beneath the moon's soft, glimmering tape,
Whispers weave the fabric of fate.
Glistening fins in twilight's glow,
Carry songs of the deep below.

In every splash, a haunting voice,
Entwined with fate's unseen choice.
The ocean's heart holds every sound,
In watery depths, wonders abound.

The Mysterious Glow of Dusk

As daylight wanes, the sky ignites,
With shades of purple, pink, and sights.
The sea embraces the fading light,
A dance of dreams that bids goodnight.

Golden flickers on the tide,
Whispers secrets that abide.
In twilight's hush, reflections play,
A world transformed in dusk's ballet.

The horizon drips with molten gold,
As stories shyly yet unfold.
In shadows deep, the sea does glow,
With mysteries only night can show.

Stars emerge as the sun dips low,
Guiding fish where currents flow.
In the depths, a soft embrace,
Cradling all in nature's grace.

With every wave, a laugh, a woe,
Underneath the mystic glow.
The nightingale sings to the sea,
Of ancient dreams that long to be.

Threads of Gloom Underwater

In currents thick with threads of gloom,
Each shadow grows, a silent tomb.
A tapestry of sorrow spun,
In watery depths where light is done.

Beneath the waves, the darkness coils,
As hope retreats from ancient toils.
The mournful cries of creatures lost,
A price to pay, at what a cost!

With every ripple, stories blend,
Of battles fought, and dreams that end.
In silence wrapped, they find a way,
To bear the weight of each dark day.

In shadows deep, where fears reside,
A haunting realm, where secrets bide.
Yet through the gloom, a shimmer glows,
A sign of life that somehow knows.

Through tangled threads, a beacon bright,
A flicker of hope in endless night.
Though darkness reigns, the heart holds fast,
In undercurrents, shadows cast.

Reflections on Waves of Night

In the hush of twilight's plea,
Shadows dance upon the sea.
Whispers trace the ocean's sigh,
Stars awaken in the sky.

Gentle moonbeams lightly play,
Chasing dreams that drift away.
Ripples cradle tales once bold,
Secrets in the deep retold.

Veils of mist like silver lace,
Echoing a lost embrace.
Moments caught in twilight's weave,
Find the magic to believe.

Beyond the surf, a rush of dreams,
Softly shining, moonlit beams.
Waves of night curl 'round the shore,
Calling forth the heart's lore.

Each reflection, quiet, bright,
Guiding souls through silent night.
In the depths, we come alive,
On these waves, our spirits thrive.

Songbirds of the Enchanted Abyss

In the glade where shadows sing,
Songbirds call, their voices ring.
Feathers bright in twilight's gleam,
Weaving through a waking dream.

Beneath the boughs of ancient trees,
Whispers flutter in the breeze.
Gentle notes from wings that soar,
Carry tales through every door.

Through the labyrinth of the night,
Guided by the pale moonlight.
Melodies in harmony,
Brought to life by mystery.

In the realm where dreams entwine,
Every heart begins to shine.
Specters dance upon the air,
Echoes of a world so fair.

As the stars in silence weep,
Into slumber, all will leap.
With the songbirds leading on,
In enchanted night, we're drawn.

The Hidden Waltz of Shadows

In the corners, shadows creep,
Where the stillness dares not sleep.
Whispers float like autumn leaves,
Spinning tales that night perceives.

Underneath the moon's soft gaze,
Dancers twirl through mystic haze.
Glimmers of forgotten lore,
Echo through the twilight door.

Step by step in shadows found,
Every heartbeat, every sound.
In their waltz, we lose the light,
Merging dreams with endless night.

Every footfall tells a tale,
Of hopes fluttering like a sail.
Through the maze of twilight's bend,
Life and myth in silence blend.

In the dance of twilight grace,
Time dissolves without a trace.
Hear the hush, the quiet call,
In shadows, we rise and fall.

Elysian Tides of the Forgotten

On the shores where memories flow,
Waves of time, they ebb and grow.
Whispers of the days gone past,
Carrying the dreams amassed.

In the sands, lost tales reside,
Echoes of the heart, our guide.
Each grain speaks of love and fear,
Life's enchantments linger near.

Through the mist of what once was,
Every ripple holds a pause.
Caught between the dusk and dawn,
In this realm, we are reborn.

Raise the tides of longing's call,
In the depths, we hear it all.
Elysium's whispers softly kiss,
Moments held in twilight's bliss.

In the ocean's endless dance,
Lies the heart's forgotten chance.
As the tides recede and swell,
Time unfolds its mystic spell.

Ethereal Echoes of the Deep

Beneath the waves where silence sings,
The echoes dance on sapphire wings.
Whispers of ages, secrets entwined,
In depths of magic, where dreams unwind.

Mermaids weave through coral's glow,
Their laughter mingles, soft and slow.
Crystals shimmer in the twilight,
Each shimmer beckons with hidden light.

A shipwreck dreams in timeless grace,
With ghostly tales of a long-lost place.
Barnacles guard the secrets there,
In the salt-kissed sea, no soul to spare.

Moonlight spins its silver thread,
Guiding the lost, the dreamers fled.
In the ocean's cradle, time stands still,
Breathless wonders, yet to fulfill.

So dive, dear wanderer, take the plunge,
Embrace the mysteries, let them lunge.
For in the depths, the truth does lie,
Ethereal echoes, forever nigh.

Secrets of the Midnight Sea

In the heart of night, where shadows play,
The ocean whispers, calling the stray.
Secrets wrapped in the foam's embrace,
Every swell holds a hidden trace.

Stars above like lanterns shine,
Guiding lost souls to the divine.
Waves like mirrors reflect the sky,
Where dreams awaken and spirits fly.

The sirens sing of olden lore,
Stories of love and the lost at shore.
With every note, a tale reclaims,
Names forgotten, yet still, they remain.

Swirling mists weave in and out,
Unraveling truths buried in doubt.
In the midnight sea, all is revealed,
The heart of the ocean, a timeless field.

So linger not on the bank so high,
Embrace the night, let your heart fly.
For the secrets of the midnight sea,
Are waiting still, just for thee.

Shadows in the Water's Embrace

Beneath the surface, shadows hide,
In the water's embrace, they bide.
Ripples carry tales untold,
Of journeys vast and mysteries bold.

A flicker of light, a fleeting glance,
In this deep realm, lost souls dance.
Glimmers of hope in the darkest night,
Each shadow holds a flickering light.

The currents whisper like a song,
Echoing where the brave belong.
With gnarled roots and ancient craft,
The ocean speaks, and the heart drafts.

Bubbles rise like laughter's glee,
Creating dreams beneath the sea.
In this realm of endless grace,
Shadows weave through time and space.

So dive, dear traveler, dare to see,
The water's secrets, wild and free.
For in this embrace, all truths converge,
The shadows wait for your heart's urge.

Veil of the Tidal Mirage

On shores where land and sea collide,
A veil of mirage, the tides do hide.
Within the mists, a world so strange,
Reality bends, and dreams rearrange.

Waves like whispers caress the sand,
Tales of adventure, both grand and planned.
Merfolk's laughter echoes through air,
In this realm, all burdens bare.

The horizon beckons, a siren's call,
Promises woven in a golden thrall.
Each step taken on this fragile line,
Blurs the dimensions, intertwines.

In the moon's glow, the secrets trail,
A dance of shadows, a haunting wail.
With every pulse, the tides ignite,
Creating visions in silver light.

So follow the veil, let it guide you near,
To the shores where dreams disappear.
For within the tidal mirage's embrace,
Lies a universe, a wondrous space.

Murmurs of Forgotten Waves

In twilight's grasp, the whispers sigh,
Forgotten tales where shadows lie.
The ocean's breath, a soft embrace,
Each wave a promise, lost in space.

Beneath the foam, memories drift,
Secrets shared in ocean's gift.
The silver light, a gleaming thread,
Where wild imaginings are fed.

From distant shores, the echoes call,
With every rise, the heart can fall.
A melody from ages past,
In liquid depths, forever cast.

Through storm and calm, the waters weave,
A tapestry that won't deceive.
In every swell, a story waits,
To dance upon the ocean's gates.

When night descends and stars awake,
The waves will sing for those who break.
Their silence speaks in soothing tones,
To hearts that yearn for time alone.

Fragments of a Fathomless Dream

In velvet night, the sea does sigh,
Where moonlight drapes the sky goodbye.
A dream unfolds in hues so rare,
Among the depths, reality's snare.

Fleeting glimpses, shadows play,
In fathomless thoughts that drift away.
With every pulse, the heartbeat sways,
Lost in the dance of endless days.

Beneath the tides, the spirits hum,
In secret realms, the thoughts succumb.
Each bubble bursts like fleeting years,
Dissolving dreams in silent tears.

Time weaves a tapestry of mist,
In every fold, a longing kissed.
The dreams conspire to intertwine,
In whispered currents so divine.

Echoes ripple from shore to shore,
Drawing souls to what they adore.
In the waves' embrace, they'll find their way,
Through fragments lost, they'll learn to stay.

The Lure of the Invisible Current

A current flows beneath the light,
Invisible force, a hidden plight.
With gentle pull, it calls the brave,
To venture forth, their souls to save.

Through tangled paths where shadows play,
The current whispers, soft and gray.
In every swell, a secret yearn,
An ancient call for hearts to learn.

Beneath the waves, the truth remains,
In currents strong, our hope gains chains.
For every soul that's lost at sea,
There lies a map to set us free.

With open hearts, we heed the song,
To seek the place where we belong.
In darkness deep, the spark will shine,
A guiding force, a love divine.

Through veils of mist and shifting tide,
The lure of fate will not subside.
Each heart, a vessel on the roam,
To discover currents lead us home.

Glimpses of an Ocean's Enchantment

In morning's light, the waves unfold,
A dance of colors, bright and bold.
With every crash, a tale is spun,
Of ancient myths beneath the sun.

The water's song, a siren's call,
With magic woven into all.
Each glimmering crest holds secret dreams,
Where nature's heart forever beams.

From coral caves to sandy shore,
The ocean's charm forevermore.
In every drop, a world concealed,
In whispers soft, our lives revealed.

The salt-kissed air, a soothing balm,
In ocean's heart, we find our calm.
With every wave, we rise and bend,
In ocean's arms, we find a friend.

Through moonlit nights, the waters roam,
A promise made, to guide us home.
In glimpses bright, we'll find our song,
With every tide, we all belong.

Lurkers in the Deep Blue Veil

In shadows deep where sirens sigh,
Lost souls drift beneath the sky.
They whisper tales of ancient dread,
In haunted waves where few have tread.

Mysteries swirl in ocean's night,
With glowing eyes, they hide from light.
Tales of treasure, whispers low,
Bound by currents, secrets flow.

A flicker here, a shadow there,
The lurking depths, a heavy lair.
Beneath the foam, a world unseen,
In twilight's grasp, the darkling green.

Yet brave of heart may seek the truth,
In tangled nets of time, forsooth.
They'll chase the whispers, heed the call,
When night descends, they'll risk it all.

For courage sought in depths so wide,
Reveals the magic that does bide.
The lurkers weave the tales we know,
As night gives way to undertow.

Secrets of the Eldritch Waters

The moonlit tide, a secret kept,
Where ancient sorrows quietly slept.
Waves that dance upon the shore,
Hide mysteries of evermore.

In whispers soft, they speak of fate,
Of journeys lost, of love and hate.
Ghostly ships on the horizon gleam,
Caught between the wake and dream.

Fathoms thick with legends old,
Stories in briny depths enfold.
A shipwreck's song, a mermaid's tear,
Echoes linger, always near.

Through moon's embrace, the waters sigh,
As silent watchers drift and fly.
Secrets tangled in kelp and sand,
Await the brave with open hand.

For those who dare the depths profound,
May find the truths that long were bound.
Eldritch waters hold the key,
To worlds unseen, forever free.

Fragments of the Enchanted Depth

In depths where dreams and shadows blend,
Fragments of magic twist and bend.
Buried treasures, shards of light,
Hidden deep in the silent night.

In coral gardens, colors soar,
Whispers echo from the ocean floor.
A flicker of hope, a spark of grace,
In the watery arms, we find our place.

Through the kelp, a pathway winds,
Leading seekers of heart and minds.
Each wave a tale, each ripple a sign,
Across the sea, destinies intertwine.

The water glows with ancient runes,
Carving stories beneath the moons.
With every dive into the abyss,
A fragment beckons, a watery kiss.

In echo's cradle, magic sleeps,
Guarded fiercely, the ocean keeps.
Fragments call through the silver streams,
Embracing those who dare to dream.

Beyond the Whispering Waves

Beyond the waves, where secrets dwell,
The ocean sings a haunting spell.
With salty breeze, the stories flow,
In silken tones, the legends grow.

Whispers rise like mist at dawn,
Of sailors lost and battles drawn.
In every crash, in every foam,
A heartbeat echoes, calling home.

Glimmers dance in twilight's embrace,
Each ripple holds a gentle trace.
Of hopes that float on currents strong,
Where weary heartbeats sing along.

The ebb and flow of time and tide,
Reveal the dreams that we still hide.
For every wave that kisses shore,
Prompts us to seek and to explore.

Beyond the horizon, a world awaits,
To brave the seas and open gates.
With courage fair, let hearts be bold,
To find the wonders yet untold.

Mysterious Murmurs Beneath the Shell

In ocean's grasp, where secrets dwell,
Lies a world enthralled by a whispered spell.
Soft voices call from the depths below,
Echoes of stories that yearn to flow.

With shells as doors to the sea's own heart,
Each tide reveals a forgotten part.
A dance of pearls in shimmering light,
Guarding the dreams of the quiet night.

Beneath the surface where shadows roam,
Murmurs of finding a long-lost home.
Let the waves cradle the tales of yore,
Unlock the magic, seek evermore.

Drifting gently on whispering air,
Lures the brave souls who venture with care.
What secrets wait in the briny deep?
In the hush of twilight, the ocean weeps.

So listen close, for the tales arise,
From coral chambers, kissed by the skies.
In the dance of the tide, the whispers blend,
Mysterious murmurs that never end.

Realm of Whispering Shadows

In the twilight's cloak, shadows waltz,
Holding secrets, hidden vaults.
The trees lean close, in softest sighs,
Whispers float under starlit skies.

Beneath the moon's watchful gaze and glare,
Shadows beckon with tales to share.
A realm where echoes of laughter sing,
And forgotten dreams take graceful wing.

Each rustle of leaves tells a tale anew,
Of past enchantments, both dark and true.
Ghostly forms of the lost and found,
In twilight's realm, the magic's profound.

The night unveils a silken thread,
Binding the tales that wish to spread.
With every gust, shadows entwine,
In a realm where the stars align.

So step with care, let your heart lead on,
Into the night, where fears are gone.
For in the whispers that dance so low,
Lie the truths the world may never show.

Tides of Forgotten Echoes

Against the shore where moments freeze,
Tides of echoes ride the breeze.
Whispers of time in the salty air,
Remind of dreams that linger there.

Each wave a message from days of old,
Stories of love and fortunes bold.
In the ebb and flow, the past unfolds,
Tales of glory, both warm and cold.

With every crest, the memories rise,
Hushed by the moon, 'neath watchful skies.
The ocean's pulse, a rhythmic beat,
Holds forgotten truths, bittersweet.

Salty winds carry ghostly charms,
Tracing the paths through the water's arms.
Yet in the stillness, a promise gleams,
For tides recede, revealing dreams.

So seek the shores where the echoes play,
For whispers of night will guide the way.
In the dance of the sea, souls unite,
Amidst the tides, find hope's new light.

Enigmas of the Nocturnal Sea

Deep in the hush of the velvet night,
Lies a realm cloaked in silver light.
The ocean stirs with a quiet song,
Where enigmas whisper, mysterious and strong.

Beneath the waves, secrets lie still,
Wrapped in shadows of the moonlit chill.
Tales of voyagers lost at sea,
And siren songs' allure, wild and free.

With every ripple, a story unfolds,
Of treasures hidden and rich, untold.
Phantom ships sail through the fog and foam,
Guided by stars that lead them home.

In the dark canvas of the ocean's depths,
Lurk ancient spirits that hold their breaths.
Guardians of wisdom, of sorrow and cheer,
Echoing tales for those who dare near.

So let the night cradle your fears away,
And follow the mysteries the sea will play.
For in the warmth of the stars' embrace,
Lies the promise of an enchanted place.

Flickers of Forgotten Lore

In shadows deep where whispers dwell,
The stories weave, a timeless spell.
Each flicker glows of ages past,
A lantern's light, its glow holds fast.

A tapestry of hope and fear,
Threads of magic linger near.
With every tale, the heart ignites,
In the silence, lost delight.

From dusty tomes, the pages sigh,
The secrets shared, they won't deny.
In every word, a world bestowed,
Flickers of lore in shadows flowed.

So gather 'round, and listen close,
The echoes of the ancient prose.
For in the night, the shadows dance,
As forgotten tales take their chance.

With every spark, a dream takes flight,
In the heart of dark, you'll find the light.
Flickers dim, yet brightly stir,
The timeless truth within their blur.

Songs of the Starlit Waters

The river sings a silver tune,
Beneath the gaze of the crescent moon.
Each ripple holds a secret fair,
As starlit dreams drift through the air.

With every wave, a story flows,
Of ancient realms where magic grows.
The waters dance with gleaming grace,
A shimmering light, a soft embrace.

The echoes of the night align,
In harmony, the worlds entwine.
A lullaby of waves will weave,
In dreamy depths, we believe.

From dusk till dawn, the waters play,
A symphony that sweeps away.
With winds that carry melodies,
Their songs will dance on evening's breeze.

In starlit moments, hearts will find,
The whispered dreams that tide entwined.
For in the flow, our spirits soar,
Songs of the waters forevermore.

Mysteries Beneath the Moonlit Wave

Beneath the wave, in twilight's glow,
Where secrets hide, and currents flow.
The moonlit tide holds tales untold,
Of shadows deep, and silver cold.

With whispers soft, the sea unveils,
A bounty rich of ancient tales.
The mysteries beneath the veil,
In every swell, a story frail.

The mermaids sing of dreams gone by,
While starlit hosts drift through the sky.
In depths of dark, the echoes loom,
Where shadows play and spirits bloom.

Through liquid dreams, the heart will wade,
In dances light, where memories fade.
The waves will quilt the untold fate,
As moonlit whispers resonate.

From every tide, a secret gleaned,
In every drop, a wish redeemed.
Beneath the waves, we drift and weave,
Mysteries waiting to believe.

In the Company of Silhouetted Dreams

In twilight's brush, the dreams arise,
Silhouetted 'neath painted skies.
With every thread, a vision spun,
A tapestry where heartbeats run.

In company of softest sighs,
We chase the tales that never die.
For in the night, our spirits gleam,
Bound together, lost in dream.

The shadows dance on whispered air,
Illuminating hopes laid bare.
In fractured light, the visions blend,
As time suspends, and hearts will mend.

Through flickered lights and muted sounds,
We find the magic all around.
In every breath, a promise made,
In dreams' embrace, we won't betray.

So let the night, with arms enfold,
As stories weave, both brave and bold.
In silhouetted dreams we soar,
Together bound forevermore.

Chiaroscuro Dreams of the Ocean Floor

In the depths where shadows dance,
Whispers of the tides advance,
Secrets held in shifting sand,
Echoes weave a mystic strand.

Moonlight spills on surfaces bright,
Casting spells in silver light,
Chasing dreams beneath the waves,
Where the silence softly saves.

Corals bloom in vibrant hues,
A symphony of muted blues,
Fishes dart with graceful flair,
In this world of hidden care.

Glimmers spark in water's flow,
Like forgotten tales of woe,
Each crest a story yet untold,
In shadows deep and currents bold.

Beneath the vast, eternal dome,
Life thrives in a liquid home,
As stars gleam from above the tide,
In this realm where dreams abide.

Sirens of the Night's Embrace

Underneath the velvet sky,
Whispers of the sea float by,
Enchanting notes on breezes ride,
Calling hearts to the ocean's wide.

Silver beams on ripples dance,
Drawing forth a daring glance,
In the hush of night's allure,
Promises that feel so pure.

Melodies from shadows call,
Luring souls to rise and fall,
With each wave a haunting plea,
Sirens sing of wild dreams free.

Glance behind the foam and mist,
Find the magic in the twist,
A story woven, tight and clear,
In the night, a spell to steer.

So let the tides your heart embrace,
In timeless waves, find your place,
For love and wonder intertwine,
In the ocean, dreams align.

Glimmers of Silken Nightfall

As dusk enfolds the quiet sea,
Stars awake, a tapestry,
Threads of silver, soft and light,
Spin their magic through the night.

Whispers ride on gentle breeze,
Carrying tales from ancient seas,
Each glimmer speaks in muted tones,
Softer than the evening's moans.

Silken waves caress the shore,
Drawing dreams forevermore,
In this realm of peace and grace,
Find the shadows, find your place.

Deep beneath, the secrets sleep,
Guarded by the ocean deep,
Softly now, they hint and tease,
On the winds, a flowing breeze.

So let the night its magic weave,
In every breath, believe, believe,
For in the dark, a light will rise,
In glimmers found beneath the skies.

Fantasies in a Watercolor Abyss

In the deep, hues blend and swirl,
Stories painted, dreams unfurl,
Each stroke a wish, a whispered sigh,
In the depths where colors lie.

Cerulean depths, a canvas wide,
Blending with the twilight tide,
Brushes dipped in ocean's hue,
Crafting worlds that feel so true.

Gentle creatures glide and weave,
In this realm, we're free to dream,
Every wave a stroke unexplored,
Tales of wonder, love restored.

With each ripple, life appears,
Drawing forth our hopes and fears,
In this watercolor embrace,
Find the magic, find your place.

So dive deep into the abyss wide,
Let your heart be your guide,
For in this sea of dreams divine,
The wonders of the soul entwine.

Nightfall's Unexpected Wanderers

As shadows stretch across the glade,
Mysterious figures start to parade.
With whispers soft like a gentle sigh,
They move through twilight, where secrets lie.

The moonlight dances on their cloaked forms,
Guiding their path through magical storms.
With eyes like stars, they see the unseen,
Carving stories where they've always been.

Among the trees, their laughter rings,
A melody woven with magic strings.
Beneath the boughs, where darkness swells,
They spin their tales, crafting spells.

In the stillness, magic unfurls,
As unseen wanderers twirl and whirl.
They weave the night into wonders bright,
Lending their dreams to the silver light.

So when the dusk begins to fall,
Listen closely to night's silent call.
For in the shadows, where dreams take flight,
Lie the wanderers of the endless night.

The Unseen Guardians of the Coral Realm

Beneath the waves, where colors blend,
Silent protectors watch and defend.
In coral castles of vibrant hue,
They tend to the sea, both old and new.

Armed with secrets of ocean deep,
In currents, their ancient promises keep.
With scales that shimmer like stars above,
They guard the realm with their endless love.

Gentle as whispers, fierce as the tide,
They weave through the reefs, like a ghostly guide.
Each flick of a tail, a song they sing,
From the depths of the sea, gift of the spring.

In hidden crevices, life blooms and thrives,
Where unseen guardians nurture our lives.
With eyes like lanterns, they light the way,
A dance of the ocean, night into day.

So should you wander where corals gleam,
Know in the shadows, there's magic, it seems.
For in the depths, unseen yet so real,
Lie guardians rare, with an ancient feel.

Phantoms Beneath the Shining Waves

In glistening depths where shadows creep,
Phantoms whisper secrets, dark and deep.
As the sun casts rays, they fade away,
Hidden in currents where dreams often sway.

With glimmering eyes like the moonlit tide,
They dance through waters, where mysteries hide.
Each flicker of light, a story untold,
Of adventure and wonder, forever bold.

Among the sands, in silence they glide,
Ethereal beings, the ocean's pride.
With echoes of laughter, they weave through the spray,
A hauntingly beautiful, luminous ballet.

When the tide turns low and the stars are bright,
The phantoms awaken from slumbering night.
In the shimmering waves where the sea breezes blow,
They bring forth the magic, a gentle glow.

So listen, dear dreamer, to the ocean's breath,
For beneath the waves lies a world of depth.
With phantoms dancing in the moon's silver beams,
They beckon you softly to share in their dreams.

Dance of the Luminous Fable

In twilight's embrace, a tale begins,
With whispers of magic on soft, hushed winds.
From dusk till dawn, the stories unfold,
A dance of the fable, both new and old.

With luminescent glow, the night takes flight,
As shadows entwine in the silver light.
Each flickering spark is a dream set free,
Embracing the rhythm, lost in the sea.

Among the stars, where wishes reside,
The fable dances, with nowhere to hide.
In the tapestry woven by time's gentle hand,
The stories of old, like grains of sand.

With laughter and joy, the nightbirds sing,
A chorus of hope that the dawn will bring.
With each whispered line, the fable swells,
A narrative cherished that softly dwells.

So let us gather as the night draws near,
And join in the dance, casting away fear.
For in the luminous fable, we'll find our way,
Guided by dreams till the break of day.

Views from a Luminous Depth

In the depths where shadows play,
A glow will find its way,
Through tangled weeds and drifting sand,
A mystery we cannot understand.

With each flicker, secrets rise,
Like whispers hid from eager eyes,
The dance of light in sunken caves,
Guides the brave, and chills the knaves.

A shimmering path entwined with fate,
Calls to hearts that hesitate,
To plunge into the azure dreams,
Where nothing's ever what it seems.

Rays of wonder weave and dart,
Each beam a tale that sways the heart,
In luminous depths, we seek our song,
Among the soft and serene throng.

Yet shadows linger, old and wise,
From tucked-away and ancient skies,
They guard the truths we hold so dear,
In the luminous depths, faced with fear.

Hues of Gloom beneath the Waves

In cerulean depths where silence dwells,
Hues of gloom weave ancient spells,
Mariners lost in dreams of dread,
Haunted by the whispers of the dead.

Through kelp and coral, shadows sweep,
Secrets buried deep in sleep,
The ocean's heart, a heavy sigh,
Where forgotten hopes and memories lie.

The silent currents, cold and stark,
Guide the way through realms so dark,
With every pulse, a woeful tune,
And echoes call beneath the moon.

Embrace the weight of whispered fears,
As storms brew up through salty tears,
The hues of gloom, a somber sea,
Hold tales of what's not meant to be.

Yet, within the dark's enticing grasp,
A flicker shines with gentle clasp,
Hope glimmers through the sullen shade,
Beneath the waves, the dreamer swayed.

Enigmas of the Midnight Current

Where currents dance in midnight's grace,
Mysterious forces interlace,
A riddle woven through the tide,
Adventures wait where secrets hide.

The deep sea's breath, a haunting call,
Whispers carried, rise and fall,
Each wave a note of long-lost lore,
Echoing tales from sacred shore.

Trinkets gather in a sailor's chest,
From battles fought and quests unblessed,
The power of stars, a compass true,
Leads the way where few pursue.

In every swirl of liquid night,
Enigmas twirl; the spirits take flight,
The midnight current flows and bends,
A tapestry of time transcends.

Adrift in dreams of brine and foam,
We find a new kind of home,
Through hidden paths of darkened brine,
Seek the treasures, yours and mine.

The Dreamscape of the Dark Sea

The dark sea breathes a dreamlike haze,
Where shadows dance in languid ways,
A canvas painted fierce and bold,
With mysteries that have yet to unfold.

Night's veil cloaks the tides' embrace,
While silken whispers swell and trace,
The echoing years held tight in sleep,
In depths where even secrets weep.

Glimmers tease from depths below,
The pulse of fate in ebb and flow,
Guiding souls through darkened dreams,
Where nothing lives while all redeems.

Phantoms' laughter under the waves,
Hold the stories of forgotten braves,
They charm the night with shimmering call,
In the dreamscape where shadows stall.

So dare to venture, take the plunge,
Let the waves your thoughts expunge,
For in the depths of the dark sea's hold,
A world awaits, new and old.

Whispers of the Moonlit Abyss

In the depths where shadows play,
Whispers echo, soft as clay.
Moonlight drapes the ocean's bed,
Secrets linger, softly said.

Tales of ships and lost/forgot,
In silence, stories over-wrought.
Echoes of the night's embrace,
Breathe the dreams of time and space.

Flickering lights beneath the tide,
Curious spirits gently glide.
Their laughter weaves a silent song,
To the depths where they belong.

Ripples speak of ancient lore,
As luminescent fish explore.
In this realm of shadowy grace,
Mysteries drift in vast embrace.

The moon above, a watchful guide,
Leading wanderers of the tide.
Beneath the waves, a world unseen,
In whispers soft, the night's serene.

Shadows Dancing in the Coral Deep

In coral gardens, vibrant and bright,
Shadows twirl in the soft moonlight.
Waves carry secrets, old and wise,
Beneath the surface, magic lies.

Tentacles sway like dancers' grace,
Chasing the currents in this place.
Colors clash in a splendid show,
Life breathes deep where few dare to go.

Fishes dart, with glimmers of gold,
In this hidden world, stories unfold.
A symphony plays in silence profound,
In the heartbeat of the sea, it's found.

Amidst the reefs, the shadows play,
In harmony where legends sway.
They whisper dreams of dusk to dawn,
In the waters, eternity's song.

Elusive forms, both gentle and wild,
In a dance of colors, nature's child.
The coral deep, a realm divine,
In whispered tones, the shadows shine.

Reflections of a Twilight Sea

Twilight paints the horizon wide,
With colors where secrets abide.
Reflecting dreams on the water's face,
A canvas of time, a sacred space.

Silhouettes of ships, sails unfurled,
Surrendered to waves, they dance and twirled.
Echoes of laughter drift on the breeze,
Carried by tales of the restless seas.

As stars awaken in the dusk's embrace,
The moon finds joy in its silver lace.
Rippling whispers in the quiet night,
Guide the wanderers till morning's light.

Reflections shimmer, flicker, and sway,
In twilight's grace, the world turns gray.
Mysteries blend where the sky meets the sea,
In the twilight's breath, we long to be.

A journey begun on these whispered waves,
Guided by love that the ocean saves.
With every tide, new stories take flight,
In the reflections of the fading light.

Elusive Creatures in the Mystic Tide

In the depths where shadows slip,
Elusive creatures twist and dip.
Threads of silver, glimmers bright,
Dance in currents, soft as light.

From the murky depths, they emerge,
In mystic tides, their spirits surge.
Glimmers of secrets, they unfold,
Ancient stories, forever told.

Fins that flash, in colors rare,
Sculpting art in the salty air.
They hide in the folds of the ocean's shroud,
Mystery cloaked in a watery crowd.

A siren's call, in the breeze it sways,
Tempting sailors to dance and play.
But deep in the waves, a warning swells,
Where magic thrives, and mystery dwells.

As the tide pulls back, they slip away,
Elusive spirits, forever at play.
In the heart of the sea, they dance and glide,
Lost in the rhythm of the mystic tide.

Echoes of the Enchanted Lagoon

In the heart of the forest deep,
Where mossy shadows quietly creep,
The waters shimmer with a glow,
Whispering secrets only they know.

Beneath the cypress, dreams take flight,
Under the watch of twinkling night,
A melody spirals, soft and sweet,
Echoes of magic where the wild things meet.

The lilies dance on a silken breeze,
A lullaby carried through ancient trees,
Each ripple sings of a tale long spun,
Of heroes lost and battles won.

Moonlight weaves through the silvery mist,
Curling around a forgotten tryst,
A sigh of longing, a breath of lore,
Calling to spirits who wander evermore.

So linger here, as shadows play,
In the enchanted lagoon, let your heart sway,
For in these waters, dreams entwine,
And all who listen shall surely find.

Secrets of the Twilight Depths

In the twilight, whispers roam,
Beneath the waves, they call it home,
Where sunlight dances on sapphire swell,
Secrets hidden in the ocean's shell.

Mysterious currents pull the heart,
From the surface, where we depart,
Tales of mermaids and lost ships sing,
Of treasures guarded by the ocean's ring.

Fishing for echoes in twilight's hue,
Dreams like fish slip fleeting through,
In the depths where shadows blend,
Whispers of the ancients never end.

Glimmers of silver, threads of fate,
Woven in ripples that softly translate,
The voices of those who dared to dive,
In twilight, the forgotten come alive.

So venture forth, brave hearts, take heed,
Listen closely, for passion's seed,
In the twilight depths, we find our way,
To the enchanted secrets that guide our day.

Flickering Lights Beneath the Waves

Under the surface where dreams collide,
Flickering lights in the twilight slide,
Dancing fish in a liquid ballet,
Sway to the rhythm, come what may.

A lantern glow from the seaweed bed,
Patterns of amber beneath your tread,
With every pulse, a story unfolds,
Of shimmering wonders and briny golds.

The ocean hums a hypnotic tune,
To the cadence of stars and the watchful moon,
Rippling twinkles echo a song,
In the depths, the world feels right and wrong.

A hidden world where time stands still,
Where adventurers linger to test their will,
Waves curl softly, in emerald grace,
Flickering lights guide to a secret place.

So dive into the unknown, oh wanderer bold,
Where tales of the ocean's heart are told,
In flickering lights, let your spirit sway,
For beneath the surface, magic holds sway.

The Silent Call of Dusk's Embrace

As the day fades into twilight's hold,
The sky adorns itself with gold,
A silent call, soft and clear,
Cradled in shadows, gathering near.

Underneath the reaching boughs,
Time breathes gently, pauses, bows,
Birds whisper secrets on the wing,
While echoes of dusk begin to sing.

The world slows down, a tranquil sigh,
Stars awaken in the velvet sky,
Each flicker holds a promise made,
In dusk's embrace, worries fade.

A tapestry woven of light and gloom,
Soft petals fall to the earth's sweet womb,
The night hums low, a lullaby fair,
As dreams converge in the twilight air.

So pause, dear friend, and heed the call,
In the silence, come one, come all,
For dusk holds magic, a gentle grace,
In the sweet, silent call of night's embrace.

Tales from the Deep's Lament

In the depths where shadows curl,
Secrets of sunlight twirl,
Whispers of sailors long departed,
Echoes of dreams once uncharted.

Bubbles rise like ancient sighs,
Where the lost and lonely lie,
Waves cradle their watery bed,
Tales of sorrow left unsaid.

Ghostly shadows, feeble light,
Tales of woe in the night,
Mermaids weep and moonbeams glow,
In the sea's dark undertow.

The tide sighs with aged grace,
Yearning for a gentle trace,
Of laughter that once filled the sea,
Now lost in the depths, set free.

And so the tale wears on, it weaves,
In foam and froth, the spirit grieves,
For each wave carries a fragment torn,
A lament of the sea, forlorn.

Ghostly Imprints on a Silvered Surface

On the mirror's edge they dance,
Reflections caught in a glance,
Fingers of mist softly trace,
Ghostly imprints time can't erase.

Once vibrant eyes, now pale as dust,
In silence lost, in shadows must,
The laughter fades, a fleeting breath,
Caught in the grasp of lingering death.

With every shimmer in the glass,
A story breathes, a tale of past,
Of moments held like whispered dreams,
Now locked in time, or so it seems.

A breath of wind, a tender touch,
As spirits call, they long for much,
To be remembered, to be seen,
In reflections where they've been.

So glance again, and you might find,
The echoes of the lost entwined,
In ghostly imprints soft and clear,
Their whispered tales for all to hear.

Lurkers in the Depths of Dusk

Beneath the cloak of evening's veil,
Softly slips a whispered tale,
Creatures dwell in shadows deep,
In secrets dark, their secrets keep.

The murmur of the twilight air,
Hints of magic woven rare,
Lights that flicker, shapes that sway,
Lurkers watching, night and day.

A rustle here, a sigh nearby,
The stars observe from up on high,
As creatures blend with twirling night,
In mystery, they seek their flight.

With every heartbeat, every breath,
The silence thickens, courting death,
Yet fear not those who linger near,
For in their depths, all truths appear.

So tread with care, and heed their call,
In dusk's embrace, we are all small,
For lurking shadows hold the key,
To the wonders of the night, set free.

The Haunting of the Shimmering Veil

Through a veil of shimmering light,
Whispers beckon in the night,
A world unseen, yet so close near,
Haunting echoes whisper clear.

With every shimmer, tales unfold,
Of love and loss, of brave and bold,
A dreamlike realm where spirits play,
In twilight's grasp, they dance and sway.

The veil, a barrier ever thin,
Hides the secrets lost within,
In moments caught between the years,
Haunting melodies, woven tears.

Embrace the chill that lingers low,
For every shadow has a glow,
A story weaves from dusk to dawn,
In haunted paths where dreams are drawn.

So step with care, tread light and true,
For shimmering veils hold worlds anew,
In the haunting's gentle touch,
We find the light that means so much.

Secrets Adrift in the Abyss

In shadows where the waters twine,
A whispered secret lies in brine.
Beneath the waves, the whispers dwell,
Carried forth by the ocean's spell.

Unfathomed truths, a hidden lore,
Clinging tightly to the ocean's floor.
In darkness deep where few have sought,
A history lost, a treasure caught.

Tales of sailors, shipwrecked dreams,
Echo softly in muted streams.
Each ripple guards a sacred past,
In the abyss, their shadows cast.

Yet glimmers of hope in murky depths,
Awake the heart with silent breaths.
The ocean's heart does beat and sigh,
With every secret that drifts by.

So heed the call of the darker sea,
For in the depths, lies destiny.
Among the currents, fate does weave,
A tapestry that none believe.

Spectres of the Coral Garden

Where coral blooms in vibrant hues,
The spectres dance with ancient views.
Beneath the sunlit azure waves,
They weave their tales, the lost and brave.

With tendrils swaying, spirits glide,
Through gardens where the lost abide.
Each flicker of a ghostly fin,
Bears witness to the life within.

Their laughter echoes in the tide,
A symphony that none can hide.
In every crevice, every bend,
The coral blooms, and dreams ascend.

With every visit, more they find,
The stories of the past entwined.
In spectral glow, the garden thrives,
Each pulse of life, a memory survives.

So wander here, where beauty reigns,
Among the coral, loss and gains.
For in this garden, one can see,
The legacy of eternity.

Phantoms in the Floating Tide

Upon the waves, the phantoms play,
As twilight bleeds into the day.
They dance on foam like whispered dreams,
A tapestry of silver seams.

With gauzy veils, they twirl and sway,
In moonlit whispers of the bay.
Each phantom holds a tale so dear,
Of love and loss, both far and near.

The tide, it carries voices soft,
Of souls that linger, drift and loft.
In every glimmer on the sea,
A memory calls, beckoning me.

Yet wander not where shadows creep,
For secrets lie in depths so steep.
They pull you close with siren's song,
In floating tides, where you belong.

So listen close to whispers' chime,
As phantoms weave through sands of time.
Their stories linger, softly glide,
In every wave, the floating tide.

The Siren's Haunting Glow

In twilight's grasp, the waters gleam,
A siren sings of lost esteem.
Her haunting glow, a cruel delight,
A melody that haunts the night.

With eyes like stars in velvet skies,
She weaves a web of soft goodbyes.
Each note she strikes, a heart ensnares,
Enticing dreams, igniting cares.

Amid the waves, her whispers flow,
A call to those who dare to go.
In depths where shadows intertwine,
She beckons forth, your soul's design.

Yet heed the warning of her call,
For many have met their destined fall.
In rapture's grip, the brave may drown,
While others wear her luring crown.

So wander close, but tread with care,
For sirens' songs can trap the air.
In haunting glow, she finds her prey,
Forever lost in shadows' sway.

Shadows of Enchantment and Illusion

In whispered woods where shadows creep,
A magic hidden, secrets deep.
With every rustle, spell is cast,
And time slips by, too quick, too fast.

Beneath the boughs, a dance of light,
In every corner, dreams take flight.
Yet caution lingers in the air,
For sweet delights can lead to snare.

The moonlit brook, a silken thread,
Entwines the thoughts inside your head.
It murmurs tales of brave and bold,
Of hearts entwined and myths retold.

A flicker here, a spark of green,
In shades of night, what might have been.
With every step, the path will wind,
While shadows weave and stars unwind.

So heed the call of night so clear,
For magic dances ever near.
In shadows soft, the truth is found,
A world of wonders, deeply bound.

Celestial Phantoms in the Depths

Beneath the stars, the waters sigh,
Where phantom whispers swim and fly.
In silver waves, the secrets blend,
As constellations softly bend.

In every ripple, stories weave,
Of dreams once held, now hard to leave.
The moon's embrace, a gentle guide,
In depths of night, our fears reside.

With every plunge beneath the veil,
A glimpse of worlds where spirits sail.
They shade the waters, lost and free,
In cosmic dances, endlessly.

Yet wandering hearts must stay aware,
Of shadows lurking in the glare.
For what you seek may lead astray,
In quiet depths where phantoms play.

So trust your heart, and watch the tide,
For cosmic truths cannot be denied.
Embrace the night and jump right in,
Where celestial phantoms start to spin.

The Gloomy Ballad of Lost Hues

In shades of gray, the shadows weep,
For colors lost in silence deep.
The sun once bright, now veiled in blight,
Leaves echoes dark by fading light.

Once danced in fields of vibrant gold,
Now memories fade, stories untold.
The sky weeps blue in mournful sighs,
As twilight falls, and daylight dies.

The trees stand bare, their whispers hushed,
In sorrow's grip, the world is crushed.
Yet through the gloom, a hope remains,
In every drop, the heart regains.

So sing the ballad, light the spark,
For dreams reside within the dark.
The hues may fade, but never fear,
For colors bloom again each year.

Take heart, dear friend, and look around,
For beauty waits, though lost is found.
In every shadow, light will break,
And from the depths, new hues will wake.

Charmed Currents of the Unknown

In twilight's grasp, where secrets flow,
The currents pull, the unknown grow.
With every churn of water's hand,
A journey starts on shifting sand.

Where twilight weaves a mystic tale,
The rivers pulse, the lanterns sail.
In every splash, a story stirs,
Of ancient lands and whispered furs.

Through hidden trails where dreams are spun,
In moonlit paths, we chase the sun.
With each embrace of shadowed light,
The currents guide through the starlit night.

So tread with care, for paths are veiled,
In charmed currents, wisdom hailed.
What waits beyond will soon unfold,
In whispered winds, the brave, the bold.

Dive deep, dear friend, and trust the flow,
For magic hides where few just go.
In currents strong, our fates entwine,
In the unknown, we learn to shine.

www.ingramcontent.com/pod-product-compliance
Ingram Content Group UK Ltd.
Pitfield, Milton Keynes, MK11 3LW, UK
UKHW021319280125
4330UKWH00005B/324